THE
FIFTH PRINCIPLE

Simple Steps To Super Success

STUDY. DO. TEACH.

THE
FIFTH PRINCIPLE

The Secret To Network Marketing Greatness

MICHAEL S. CLOUSE

Nexera™LLC Publishers *Lynnwood, Washington U.S.A.*

THE FIFTH PRINCIPLE
Published by Nexera™LLC

© 2003 by Michael S. Clouse

International Standard Book Number: 0-9635949-8-2

ALL RIGHTS RESERVED

Nexera™LLC
18423 – 12th Avenue West
Lynnwood, WA 98037-4900 U.S.A.

v@nexera.com
www.nexera.com/v

U.S.A. 1 888 639 3722 International +1 425 774 4264

10 9 8 7 6 5 4 3 2

ADVANCED PRAISE
FOR THE FIFTH PRINCIPLE

"When Michael asked me to review *The Fifth Principle*, I jumped at the opportunity. I devoured it—cover to cover—TWICE!

That night I shared just one concept from his book on a conference call. As a result, our team went on to set a new weekly record for sales and sponsoring!

The Fifth Principle is now recommended reading for every new member on our team. One of the best books on Network Marketing in years!"

Art Jonak
CEO, MLMPlayers.com

"Follow Michael's sage advice shared throughout this gem of a book, and you'll dramatically increase the amount of successful associates and leaders within your organization! Promote *The Fifth Principle* big-time!"

Bob Burg
Author of *Endless Referrals & Winning Without Intimidation*

"Clouse is brilliant. Everything he does is worth looking at and *The Fifth Principle* is no exception. Get it. Read it. Apply it!"

Randy Gage
Author of *How to Build a Multi-Level Money Machine*

———————————

"*The Fifth Principle* is a short, easy to read, and extremely effective book that you should get into the hands of every new distributor. In Network Marketing we all try to teach our teams how to build successful businesses, and now *The Fifth Principle* shows us a brilliant way to duplicate even faster. Do yourself, your business, and your bank account a favor—buy a case of books, or two, or three."

Orjan Saele
The European Professor of Network Marketing.
The #1 income earner in all of Scandinavia.

———————————

"Clear, simple, and just five steps. I really enjoyed reading this book."

Tom "Big Al" Schreiter
www.fortunenow.com

"Is *The Fifth Principle* great stuff? Try this test: Buy 10. Give them to your people—even and especially your business prospects—and ask each of them to read it in 24 hours. (That's easy.) At the end of your current pay-period, subtract the costs of the books from the increase in your check. Use 10 percent of that amount to buy more books. Keep doing that for one year. Then do whatever you desire for the rest of your life."

John Milton Fogg
Author of *The Greatest Networker in the World*
Founder, *greatestnetworker.com*

"*The Fifth Principle* is a 'must have' book for all distributors in Network Marketing. Because when you read and apply the principles in this book, you will be off to a 'flying start' in your new business."

Jens Ove Johannessen
Leading the largest Network
Marketing organization in Norway.
Top title in his company!

TABLE OF CONTENTS

DEDICATION

The Fifth Principle is personally, professionally, and passionately dedicated to Frank and Theresa AuCoin.

Frank and Theresa AuCoin epitomize everything that is right with our industry...and personally personify the principles contained in this book.

Frank and Theresa: It was a pleasure to be invited to Charleston, South Carolina as your special guest speaker in 1998. Today, I am truly honored to call you my friends... And I look forward to many more long conversations, well into the wee hours of the morning.

V

January, 2003

PREFACE

I have enjoyed many fortunate occurrences throughout my Network Marketing career... A chance meeting with an investigative journalist, who was looking for an expert in our industry for a story she was writing on women entrepreneurs, was given my name. Through conversation, an idea was born, and a few months later my first book, *Future Choice*, was published.

The founding Editor-in-Chief of Upline®, Mr. John Milton Fogg, was sent a review copy of *Future Choice*. He liked the book, and wrote a nice review. We spoke, and after a few conversations I took over for John as the new Editor-in-Chief of Upline®.

My first assignment at Upline® was to interview Richard Poe who had just released

Wave 3. The interview went extremely well, and soon, Mr. Poe had interviewed me for inclusion in his second book, *The Wave 3 Way to Building Your Downline*, and then a short time later for his third book, *Wave 4*.

As Master of Ceremonies, I had the opportunity to become better acquainted with Randy Gage, Tom "Big Al" Schreiter, and Art Jonak during several *Upline® Masters Weekend* conferences. Through this enhanced association, I was invited to join Tom "Big Al" Schreiter on his annual MLMCruise.com, where in November 1997 I got the chance to briefly meet two very young, and somewhat brash Networkers, Orjan Saele, and Jens Ove Johannessen, both from Oslo, Norway—both just getting started with their Network Marketing careers.

Years pass... I left Upline® to build my Networking Marketing empire, began writing a weekly column for Nexera e-News™ and focused the remainder of my time on my ever-growing speaking career. Several hundred speeches later, I was asked to speak for the first time in Sweden. The event went well—word got around—and in January, 2003, I was invited by Orjan and Jens to speak in Oslo, Norway... These are the same two Networkers I had first met on the MLM Cruise back in 1997, however, they were now quite sophisticated, very self-confident, and, yes, they were also the top distributors in the fastest growing Network Marketing company in all of Scandinavia. Apparently, the one thing these two Norwegians had discovered on that MLM Cruise—and then immediately implemented—was the awesome power of a highly duplicatable system...

I share this background information with you because it was during a brainstorming session in 1998 with Frank and Theresa AuCoin that the idea for The Fifth Principle first began to take shape. And yet it took another five years, several hundred presentations, and a bit of personal prodding by Orjan Saele (when he and his girlfriend Hilde Rismyhr were guests in our home) to convince me to write the finished book you now hold in your hands. Apparently Napoleon Hill, the author of *Think and Grow Rich* was indeed right when he wrote: "First comes thought... Then organization of that thought into ideas and plans. Then transformation of those plans into reality."

Thought. Idea. Plan. Action. Reality. Yes, it really does work!

And now it's your turn... Because if you will read, study, and then put into practice all five principles contained in this book... If you will get this book into the hands of every distributor on your team so that they too may benefit... And if you will take the time to share all that you have learned with those on your team—you too can transform your thoughts, ideas, and plans into your own living masterpiece!

All the best,

MSC

P.S. Now turn the page, and let's go to work on your future...

I

THE FIRST PRINCIPLE
GET CONNECTED – STAY CONNECTED

"Communication. It's the name of the game!"

The single-most important step you will ever take in building your Network Marketing enterprise is simply getting started.

If you want to build your organization once—and get paid on it for a lifetime—take the time to *get plugged in*, and then access the ongoing stream of information offered by your sponsor, your support team, and your company.

THE SYSTEM

In this industry everyone talks about *the system* and yet only the more successful support teams understand the awesome duplicatable power that a well-designed system offers to new distributors and established leaders alike. Indeed, *the system* will show everyone on your team a specific way to: 1) get new distributors started 2) explain when, where, and how to find prospects 3) teach distributors how to professionally present products and services to potential customers—as well as the business opportunity to prospects—and 4) be simple enough so that the cycle—or *the system*—will continue time after time, new distributor, after new distributor, as described above.

Ask your support team about *the system* they are using, and how they recommend you get started, because odds are good that *the system* is already in place, and if you follow it you can achieve any level of success you desire.

Several components of *the system* deal with how you stay connected with your sponsor, support team, and company. They include:

GENEALOGY

Your support team can play a key role in your early success if you know who they are, how they can help you, and you make it known to them that you are serious about your success—part-time or full-time—and want to be part of the team. Every distributor should have a printed list that includes his or her support team by name, location, title, and contact information. Make sure you know where you are in the organization—and that all your new distributors know too.

E-MAIL

We live in the Internet age. I believe it is now safe to say that if you are not online—while you may not end up in the bread line—you are out of the information loop. And again, because communication is the name of the game, if you are serious about Network Marketing, you need to be online.

Ask your support team how and where to get your e-mail address, then, get online, and learn how to send and receive e-mail.

WEB SITE

Today more and more companies are offering distributors their own Web Sites: www.yourcompany.com/yourname. If your company offers this service, get it as soon as possible. If your company does not offer this service, or you believe that you could "build a better mousetrap," talk with your support team first before doing anything. That "system" thing again!

ONLINE NEWSLETTER

Many leadership teams are now using e-mail to broadcast group-specific news to thousands of "wired" distributors at one time. Commonly called an e-mail blast, these time-sensitive messages should more than keep any serious Networker up to date with company news, product announcements, as well as event/

training dates and details. Make sure you subscribe to—and regularly read—the e-mail that your sponsor, support team and company sends.

VOICEMAIL

The telephone number on your business card may very well be your company approved 800 number. If your Networking business is a part-time venture and you don't want to print your home telephone number on your business card... If you have small children and would like to ensure a more professional voice answers the telephone... If your support team uses a voicemail system to distribute important information... If any of these apply to you—get voicemail. Ask your sponsor what service, if any, is being used, order it, use it, and keep the integrity of *the system* alive.

CONFERENCE CALLS

In addition to the written word—e-mail, e-zine, corporate magazine, or otherwise—many support teams offer weekly conference calls, training calls, or business opportunity calls to those on their respective teams. These calls can be a great way to stay connected—and build your empire—all from the comfort of your home-based business. Get the call-in number, along with the date and time of the call, from your sponsor or your support team, and then make sure you're listening.

LOCAL BUSINESS EVENTS

Network Marketing is a person-to-person, relationship building business. Trying to build a successful business without ever meeting with, or talking to, anyone on your team does not work long-term. Therefore, if you want to build your organization once—and get paid on it for a lifetime—you must attend the local business events. Depending on your company—and where you live in the world—these events could be held in a coffee shop, private home, restaurant, hotel conference room, or any other location that is recommended by your support team. Local business events usually take place weekly, at a regularly scheduled time. Make sure that you know where these events are taking place, and then attend as often as you possibly can.

REGIONAL BUSINESS EVENTS

In addition to the local business briefings held in your area, your support team—or local leadership—will schedule larger events on a monthly, or quarterly basis. Distributors within a certain region of the country attend these business events to learn from some of the top leaders your support team, or company has to offer. Attending these events is an absolute must *if* you want to learn from the best-of-the-best!

NATIONAL & INTERNATIONAL BUSINESS EVENTS

Just like regional events, national and international business events are simply bigger, hopefully better, and should offer even more product knowledge, along with all the how-to-do-this-business training that can be jammed into a two- or three-day event. Because this is where distributors really learn about the business—and company—they have chosen to be associated with, attending these events as soon as possible is the single best decision any distributor can make when it comes to his or her long-term likelihood for success.

BUSINESS CARDS

The sooner you have your own business cards, the sooner you will feel like you are in business. Find out from your support team what cards to order—and then order them! Follow these simple rules to keep the look and feel of your cards professional:

Do: use the cards your support team recommends—because having the same business card is part of *the system*. Include your name, e-mail address, Web Site address, and telephone number. Your home or business address is optional.

Correct:

Do not: create your own cards, or include the words e-mail, Web Site, phone...or clutter your card with too many unnecessary details.

Incorrect:

Because communication is the name of the game, every time you start someone new in your business, get them plugged in! E-mail, Web Site,

Online Newsletter, Voicemail, Conference Calls, Local, Regional, National & International Business Events, Business Cards, along with your subscription to whatever your support team and company offers. Simply make sure everyone you're working with—including you—gets, and stays, plugged in!

⋰ I ⋱

The First Principle
Get Connected – Stay Connected

II

The Second Principle
Learn Your Core Product Line

"Remember the proverb: facts tell, stories sell."

Because building your business is ultimately about moving as many products, goods, and services as you can—both inside your ever-growing empire, and to customers outside your organization as well—product knowledge does become somewhat important over time. Therefore, study one core product (those products you want everyone to use) every day, until you learn, understand, and can share all its benefits!

Now, there are two distinct ways to learn your core product line: 1) *factually*, i.e., what is it, what's in it, what's it used for, etc. and 2) *emotionally*, i.e., what are the benefits to using it. Let me explain:

FACTUALLY — STUDY THE PRODUCT

Although the facts are important to some degree, they are usually not the real reason someone buys something. If you would like to better understand what I mean, take a moment and picture in your mind one of the products you have in your home—like salad dressing, or shampoo, or soap. As you do, take the *Seven Question Test:*

1) Who made this? (manufacturer)
2) Where was it made? (actual location)
3) How long have they been in business? (what year)
4) Is this the best price available? (how do you know)
5) Is this the best value around? (compared to what)

6) Can you get a similar product for less? (do you care)

7) Why did you buy this product? (how factual is your reason)

If you apply this test to six different products you have around the house—kitchen, closet, and bathroom—you quickly begin to realize that the real reason you acquire products is more about the feeling you get, and less about: who made it, where was it made, or how long the company has been in business.

If this is true, that we tend to buy when it feels right, more than when we know everything there is to know about something—and for the most part this is true—why should you study your core product line? The answers are: 1) to build up your personal knowledge about what it is you're offering, and 2) in order to be able to intelligently answer basic questions from your customers and new distributors alike—those who simply *must* know a bit (or a lot) more before they make a purchase. However, please keep in mind even the most analytical shopper still seeks that certain "feeling" before parting with his or her hard earned cash. As a result, in addition to *factually* studying your core products, you would also do well to share the stories.

EMOTIONALLY — SHARE THE STORIES

By now you have hopefully paused long enough to take the previously mentioned *Seven Question Test*, and have come to realize that unless you were holding the actual product in your hand and could read the label, you probably failed the test. Perhaps you now understand that you also buy what you do for reasons that are not always factual, and are many times verbally difficult to describe. However, odds are good—for one reason or another—you like the products you purchase, and that is why you continue to buy them.

Now the better question is, if you were going to try to convince your co-workers, family, or friends that product "X" was a great product, and they really should be using it too, how would you go about doing this? You would share product "X" with them emotionally, by sharing the stories... The same way you recommend a restaurant: "You really should try *The Mango King*, the food is fantastic—and they have this amazing chocolate mousse dessert that just melts in your mouth..." Or, the same way you tell them about the movie you saw Saturday night: "We went to see *My Big Fat Greek Wedding*. I can't remember the last time we all laughed so hard..." Or, the same way you—perhaps without even knowing that you were recommending it—suggest that a friend take his or her vacation in the same place you recently took yours: "You have got to go to the South Island of New Zealand—it's simply the most beautiful place on earth..."

You do it all the time. You recommend something to someone without giving him or her all the facts. And if you're successful in getting your point across—thereby creating a new customer for someone—it is more often because of the tone in your voice, the look in your eyes, and your internal belief—how you *feel*—than almost any other fact. True, we do buy more easily from those we know, like, and trust. Yet even when we know, like, and trust someone, we will still buy more on the feeling of *emotion* than on any other *factual* reason. Yes, do study your core product line. However, always remember that there is a reason for the proverb: facts tell, stories sell.

So where will you learn the stories? From your company's audio, video, and print information. From reading your company's and support team's e-mail blasts. From listening to your company's and support team's conference calls. From talking with, and listening to, your customers. And by regularly attending your local, regional, national, and international business events.

Be Your Own Best Customer

More and more Network Marketing companies are now offering hundreds of products to their ever-growing customer and distributor organizations. With this in mind, the question is often asked, "Should I be buying everything my company offers?" The corporate answer is, "Yes!"

However, the real-world answer is, "You should replace those products you currently buy somewhere else with those products, goods, and services that your company distributes." This is referred to as "being your own best customer." And in Network Marketing, "being your own best customer" is just good business.

Know Your Goal

Because when everything is said and done, building your business is about moving as many products, goods, and services as you possibly can—from your company to the ultimate end user—both inside your ever-growing empire, and to customers outside your organization. Ask your support team what core products you should be purchasing: get them, use them, study them, and share the stories.

❧ II ❧

THE SECOND PRINCIPLE
LEARN YOUR CORE PRODUCT LINE

III

THE THIRD PRINCIPLE
LEARN HOW YOU ARE PAID

"Customers + distributors = long-term,
on-going income."

As we have previously discussed, you must become your own best customer. All those products, goods, and services you acquire should be ones that you actually enjoy. So too, you will need to create customers. And it is easier to recommend a restaurant, movie, or vacation spot if it has had a positive emotional effect on you. And yes, you will need to sponsor other distributors. Because if *compound interest* is the "Eighth Wonder of the World," *time leverage* is certainly the "Ninth Wonder of the World." It's true, when you discuss the benefits of building your own Network Marketing business, you too will realize: "It's about the money."

How You Are Paid – Factually

All Network Marketing companies offer some sort of "here-is-how-you-are-going-to-be-paid" plan, usually referred to as the Marketing Plan, Compensation Plan, or the Operating System. For purposes of commonality, I will simply refer to these collectively as the *plan*.

Customers

You can quickly determine how well a company might survive long-term by asking about the company's view (internal), as well as your support team's view (external), of attracting and keeping customers.

Why are outside customers so important? In some countries, having customers that are *not* distributors is one sure way to separate a legal company from an illegal company. However, regardless of whether the law requires you to have customers or not, the overall health of your business will always be determined by how easy it is to get—and keep—long-term outside customers. Here are two reasons why this is true...

People who are presented with your products, goods, and services, or presented with the opportunity of becoming distributors, or both, and decide to become customers reveal that: 1) people will actually purchase your products in the marketplace without a money-making opportunity attached to them, and 2) with outside customers, you will simply earn much more money! Because if Microsoft®, Sony®, or Erickson® only sold products internally (to employees) they could never generate the kind of income that comes from selling products, goods, and services both *internally* (to employees) and *externally* (to customers). Let me put it another way...

I love to travel. And for me, travel usually involves jet airplanes, beautiful resorts, and fine restaurants...along with, of course, a bit of sightseeing. Now the fact is being a jet pilot, resort owner, chef, or tour-guide are all honorable professions. However, regardless of how financially appealing the upside potential of those professions might be—I just want to be a customer. I don't want to own the airline, I just want to sit up front, enjoy the ride...and then be on my way to the resort, where I can bask in the warm sunshine, and then perhaps a bit later enjoy a relaxed conversation with a few good friends over a great meal. In other words, I just want to be a customer.

The airline needs customers like me. The resort, the fine restaurant, and the sightseeing company all need customers like me. And your ever-expanding empire needs customers just like me too.

The bottom line is that customers create cash. The more customers you have, the more cash you will earn. Your job is to read over your company's *plan*, ask your sponsor about the *plan*, or discover exactly how you will be paid through your support team's "getting started" process.

DISTRIBUTORS

In addition to customers, you will also need to grow your business by introducing the opportunity to other people who—for one reason or another—might be interested in: 1) a career change 2) earning some extra money, 3) creating a full-time income on a part-time schedule, or 4) making more money in a month then they currently do in a year!

Let's say that you decide on option #3 above—creating a full-time income on a part-time schedule—and that you want to create a replacement income of $5,000 per month, working 15-hours per week. According to one *plan*, the numbers would look like this:

You sponsor 5	You + 5	= 6
Who each sponsor 5	5 x 5	= 25
Who each in turn sponsor 5	25 x 5	= 125
Total distributor organization		= 156

With 156 distributors in your organization, and having taught each distributor how to find 5 customers, your monthly product sales could look like this: 156 x $100 = $15,600 per month in *internal* volume + (780 customers x $50 each) $39,000 in *external* volume, for a grand total of $55,220 in monthly (distributors + customers) volume.

Depending on the *plan*, if you were to earn 10% on your first three levels, this example would create an income of $5,522 per month! Simply by you sponsoring 5, teaching those 5 how to sponsor 5, and teaching those 25 how to sponsor 5 more—with each distributor averaging $100 per month, and managing just 5 customers each, who in turn purchases an average of $50 per month.

Now this is just one example. However, if this were your *plan*, and how you were paid, would you: 1) understand it? and 2) could you explain it to others? Make sure you take the time to study your *plan* so that both your answers will be a resounding, "Yes!" After all, if "It's about the money," you really should know where the money comes from.

Sit down with your sponsor and learn: 1) how you are paid when you sponsor a new distributor who places a product order, or signs up for a service 2) how you advance through the ranks, 3) how you will be paid at higher ranks, 4) how you are paid on customer sales, and 5) what steps you will need to take—and over what period of time—to create the business of your dreams. Because in Network Marketing, you really do determine your own destiny.

ON-GOING INCOME

In addition to the monthly income you will earn from your customer sales and distributor organization, Network Marketing promises something more: long term on-going income. The ability to do the work once, and then get paid on those same efforts many times over—possibly for years to come. For example, many times I have been asked, "How much money did you earn in your first month?" Attempting to make a point—that this business is not about how much you earn in your first month, but rather how much you earn over time from those efforts—I reply, "Well, that's hard to say exactly... You see, I'm still being paid on my first month's work."

When it comes to your *plan*, just make sure you understand this is a simple business. Because it is not how many customers you get—it's how many customers you keep, that determines your long-term on-going income. So too, it is not how many distributors you sponsor—it's how many distributors you keep, that also determines your long-term on-going income. Indeed, if you will just learn and apply your *plan*, thereby focusing on long-term on-going income in your business, everything else will take care of itself.

How You Are Paid – Emotionally

A few pages back when we discussed *The Second Principle: Learn Your Core Product Line*, I asked that you remember the proverb: facts tell, stories sell. Well, that same point applies with your *plan* as well. Yes, read your distributor manual, talk with your sponsor, and plug into your support team to learn how you are paid for customer sales, distributor sales, rank advancement, and how you can create long-term on-going income within your company's *plan*. However, when you are explaining your "here-is-how-you-are-going-to-be-paid" *plan* to a potential new distributor, please understand that again, facts tell, stories sell.

When you are giving your presentation, keep in mind that all your prospect really wants to know is: 1) what is this business all about? And then if they like what they hear, 2) can I fit this into my already too-busy life? And then lastly, if they believe there is enough of a "What's in it for me?" benefit, 3) can I do this? And the best way to answer your prospects questions—so they make the right decision to join your company—is by telling stories. Stories about other people who joined the company, used the products, goods, and services, and earned the money—and how their lives were changed for the better!

Sit down with your sponsor and review the audiotapes, videotapes, and attend the trainings. Whatever it takes for you to find out how you are paid, and how those who join you will be paid as well. Study the *plan* and the "lifestyle" stories... You know, how David and Mary bought that shiny new red Mercedes, financed their children's university education, and then retired 15-years early with a summer home in Aspen, Colorado.

⁙ III ⁙

THE THIRD PRINCIPLE
LEARN HOW YOU ARE PAID

IV

THE FOURTH PRINCIPLE
LEARN HOW YOU BUILD THE
BUSINESS

"Build it once. Get paid on it for a lifetime."

Networking Marketing should be an exact science—it isn't. The reasons are partly because of the different products, goods, and services being offered, and partly due to the countless creative ways companies come up with attempting to set themselves apart from the competition. Furthermore, a lot of the complexities can be traced right back to the very reason many of us decided to become involved in Network Marketing in the first place... We wanted to be our own boss, set our own hours, and work at our own pace. All good things to be sure, except when duplicatable simplicity of *the system* is your desired end result.

However, even with all its complications, Networking Marketing can be an easy business to get started in, to build, and to prosper from. That is, as long as we agree that our definition of *easy* is: something you can do. With this in mind, your next step in getting started is to learn all the ways the business—your business—can be built.

LEARN ALL THE WAYS

Sit down with your sponsor, support team, or local area leader, and find out how many different ways there are to build the business. When you do, you will probably learn that there is more than one way to become successful in the time you have to invest. Some of these different ways include: 1) generating retail sales, and creating preferred customers 2) building your business using one-on-one, two-on-one, home meetings, and/or formal presentations 3) utilizing business events, and trade shows, 4) the Internet, along with, of course, 5) any accepted forms of advertising. Your goal is to uncover all the different ways successful people are already building the business, and then select the way that works for you. Because if you stay within your comfort zone—what is easy to do— you will succeed quicker, because you will most likely *continue* to do that which you find, again, easy to do.

STAY INSIDE THE SYSTEM

In *The First Principle: Get Connected – Stay Connected*, I explained the concept—and benefits—of *the system*:

Indeed, *the system* will show everyone on your team a specific way to: 1) get new distributors started 2) explain when, where, and how, to find prospects 3) teach distributors how to professionally present products and services to potential customers—as well as the business opportunity to prospects—and 4) be simple enough so that the cycle—or *the system*—will continue time after time, new distributor, after new distributor.

However, when I recommend that you learn *all* the ways there are to build your business, and then choose what's right for you, I was *not* suggesting you venture outside the scope of your sponsor's, support team's, or company's established method of doing business. What I *am* suggesting is that within *the system* you will usually discover more than one way to create success. For example, to effectively build your business, you will need to find a few good prospects—and there are *several* great ways to do this. However, once those prospects are found, you still want to introduce them to the business, *and* get them started using *the system*.

Ask your sponsor about *the system* they are using, and how they recommend you get started. Because again, odds are good *the system* is already in place, and if you simply follow it, you truly can achieve any level of success you desire.

THE ENTREPRENEURIAL SPIRIT

Network Marketing often attracts those with the entrepreneurial spirit... Wanting to be their own boss, set their own hours, and work at their own pace, many of these energetic, and enthusiastic entrepreneurs want to create incomes of $10,000, $25,000, or even $100,000 per month and more! And oftentimes they want to bring into their new business a former corporate idea, strategy, or campaign that might have worked well in the past—or one they always wanted to try and didn't get the chance— that ends up sounding a little something like this: "I think if I could just change *the system* a little and do it this way, then we would really have something..."

The challenge—and it is a challenge—is that even if their way (or your way) is better, it may not work long-term. Why? Because, again, this business attracts so many energetic, and enthusiastic entrepreneurs, if everyone took their best shot at making *the system* better, in a very short period of time you would not have any system at all!

Ask yourself this question, "What do I really want?" And if your answer is you want to "Build it once, and get paid on it for a lifetime"...then warmly embrace the duplicatable simplicity of *the system* and focus your entrepreneurial spirit on building your empire! Because in Network Marketing, duplication is what success looks like.

❧ IV ❧

THE FOURTH PRINCIPLE
LEARN HOW YOU BUILD THE BUSINESS

V

The Fifth Principle
Take Action + Get Better

*"Take all-out massive action.
Get better at the game!"*

If there is a secret to success in Network Marketing, it is simply this: get connected, study your core product line, learn how you are paid, have someone successful teach you *the system*, and then take all-out massive action!

However, if your desire is to go beyond success to greatness, you will need to embrace one additional activity: get better at the game!

It's true! Those who achieve *massive* success in Network Marketing understand that there is a difference between *activity* (doing) and *acumen* (knowing how). Between *brawn* (working every waking moment) and *brains* (using *the system*). Between *ignorance on fire* (I have no idea what I am doing, but I sure am excited!), which will slowly kill your business, and *knowledge applied* (I know exactly what I am doing—and I'm doing it!), which will grow your empire.

Action alone says, "Find plenty of people to prospect." Knowledge applied asks, "What book can I read, what audio program can I listen to, or what class can I attend to teach me the skill of prospecting?"

Action alone says, "Present your products, goods, and services to as many of those prospects as you possibly can." Knowledge applied asks, "What book can I read, what audio program can I listen to, or what class can I attend to teach me the skill of presentation?"

Action alone says, "Every time one of your prospects joins you in the business, just tell them to 'Make a list of 100 people, and then go sign them all up!'" Knowledge applied asks, "What book can I read, what audio program can I listen to, or what class can I attend to teach me the skill of duplication?"

Action alone says, "Become a leader second to none." Knowledge applied asks, "What book can I read, what audio program can I listen to, or what class can I attend to teach me the skill of leadership?"

Indeed, if your desire is truly to create a Network Marketing business that—once it has been properly built—will continue to economically reward you, year after year, decade after decade, use the following four step formula:

1) EVALUATE YOUR BUSINESS

At the beginning of each month, set aside 30-minutes to review the four major areas of your business—namely prospecting, presentation, duplication, and leadership—by asking the following questions: 1) do I have plenty of prospects? 2) do I sponsor my fair share of those prospects? 3) do the prospects I sponsor duplicate *the system*? and 4) do I feel confident when it comes to my own leadership skills?

2) CHOOSE ONE AREA

Once you have considered each of the previously mentioned areas of your business, select one area to improve on over the next 30 days. Focus on: prospecting, presentation, duplication, or leadership.

3) INVEST YOUR MONEY

Go get a book, purchase a set of audiotapes/CDs, or register for a class that by its very title would suggest that it will help you "get a little better" in one area of your business: prospecting, presentation, duplication, or leadership. Translation: over the next five years, read one book per month; listen to one set of tapes per month; take one class every three months. Become a serious student of success!

4) GET EVEN BETTER

Read for 30-minutes every day—first thing in the morning, or last thing at night. Listen to an audiotape/CD for 30-minutes every day—do this while you're getting ready for the day! Take one class every three months; these classes could be—and usually are—taught by your local leaders, your support team, or your company. Repeat this same four-step process every month *until* your business, your bank account, and your life are working just the way you want.

THE PROMISE

Remember too, that anything worthwhile will take time to create... True, your Network Marketing success will usually require at least eight to ten hours per week, setting aside one Saturday per month, and investing one weekend per quarter for about three to five years—if it is your desire to replace your current full-time income. However, the great news is that if you learn, and then follow *the system*, take all-out massive action, *and* go to work on getting better at the game, you may actually be able to cut that three to five year time frame in half! A worthy reward *if* you're truly interested in achieving time and financial freedom!

So there you have it: the secret to Network Marketing greatness is knowledge applied... *Knowing* what to do—and then *doing* what you know. Taking all-out massive action *and* getting better at the game.

Therefore, if you will master The Fifth Principle, and then teach this powerful concept to all those on your team, you will be well on your way to building your own empire. Because when you apply The Fifth Principle, all the success your heart desires *is* well within your reach!

∵ V ∵

THE FIFTH PRINCIPLE
TAKE ACTION + GET BETTER

EPILOGUE

When it comes to building your business, the Greek philosopher Aristotle, who lived from 384-322 B.C., summarized it beautifully when he wrote, "The things we have to learn before we can do them, we learn by doing them." How true… And over twenty-three hundred years later, most Networkers will eventually hear that same thought put into words this way… If your *"Why?"* is strong enough, you will figure out *"How?"* Translation: if you have a clear, complete, and compelling reason *why* you are going to build your Network Marketing business, you will do whatever it takes to learn *how* to accomplish that goal somewhere along the way…

So the question is, "Do you have a clear, complete, and compelling reason *why* you are going to build *your* Network Marketing Empire?

Although your first real *why* may be, "It's about the money!", over time you will probably want to decide how much money, and what all those added earnings are for... An example might be to use some of your new capital to pay for a housekeeper, a gardener, and a nanny—they really don't cost all that much, and yet they will free up a fair amount of your time to build your business and to enjoy your life.

For me personally, I love to travel... When I'm booked as a speaker, I enjoy flying in a day or two before the event, and sometimes staying a day or two after—just to have a look around. What will you be doing with your time and financial freedom?

I enjoy being with my family... My wife, September and I have two grown children, our son Taylor who is married to Valerie, and our daughter, Ashley who is married to Aaron. Although I do travel a bit, a nice sit-down dinner at the Clouse house is almost a weekly event— as we all enjoy great food, and good times— and we often invite a few dinner guests. How about you? Do you have any desire to be the one entertaining, or would you simply prefer being entertained?

I am a collector of books... Wherever I find myself—home, the States, or abroad—not too many days will pass by before I will make my way back into a bookstore where I enjoy looking for books by the pioneers of personal development: *How to Win Friends and Influence People* by Dale Carnegie, *The Magic of Believing* by Claude M. Bristol, *As A Man Thinketh* by James Allen, *Think and Grow Rich* by Napoleon Hill, *The Richest Man in Babylon* by George S. Clason, *The Greatest Salesman in the World* by Og Mandino, or *The Magic of Thinking BIG* by David J. Schwartz just to name a few. And when I find some of these classics, I buy them, bring them to my next engagement and give them away. If you had the time and money, what would you do?

Well, if you will invest a few minutes and answer the following three questions, you'll be on your way to building your better life: 1) what would it take to get you up out of bed early in the morning? 2) what would it take to keep you up working late into the night? 3) how would you choose to live your life if you had plenty of time and financial resources available to you? Because when you answer these questions you will uncover your real reason for the money— the real reason for your life. And when you do, you will also find your *"Why?"*

So if you're ready to begin building your business and your better life: 1) take a moment and evaluate your business 2) then choose one area to improve—prospecting, presentation, duplication, or leadership 3) invest your money—go get that book, set of tapes, or register for that next class, then take action and 4) go to work on getting even better!

And if you're not sure exactly where to begin, allow me to offer the following seven suggestions: 1) subscribe to Nexera e-News™ by e-mailing your name with the word "subscribe" to add@nexera.com 2) send an e-mail to secrets@nexera.com, and I'll send you a *free* copy of our 17 page Special Report entitled, *Seven Prospecting Secrets* 3) ask your sponsor what books to read, audio programs to acquire, or what classes to attend 4) visit the <u>Your Library</u> link on nexera.com for a list of must-read books 5) visit <u>The Masters</u> link on nexera.com for a nice collection of personal development audiotapes and CDs 6) visit the <u>Success Store</u> link on nexera.com to view a selection of Network Marketing specific programs 7) review the last few pages of this book, and then order the recommended products and services listed as soon as you possibly can.

Start where you are...take all-out massive action...go to work on getting better at the game... And over time, you too can create a magnificent life!

All the best,

Michael S. Clouse
May 2003

P.S. If you have any comments on The Fifth Principle, I would enjoy reading them. Please send your e-mail to: msc@nexera.com

Master the Fundamentals in 90 Days!

prospecting, presentation, duplication, leadership

Listen to our step-by-step, connect-the-dots, build-your-business-faster audio program, and you'll learn:

1) how to get your business started right,
2) prospecting, presentation, and duplication, and
3) the secret to finding and developing leaders.

If you want to succeed in your business, listening to—and learning from—this audio training program is an absolute must!

To order yours: visit www.nexera.com/90
or call
U.S.A. 1 888 639 3722 International +1 425 774 4264

Thinking Your Way To Success

"Change your thinking and you will change your life!"

"This is the most powerful information on the mind I have ever assembled... It explains why only a few distributors succeed, *and* why far too many simply fail— and how you can use your mind to become one of the top performers in your company, build a great business, and truly live an extraordinary life! Get these CDs into the hands of every distributor you have on you team—and experience the power of *"Knowledge Applied!"*

—Michael S. Clouse

This program contains three CDs, the complete PowerPoint outline, and includes, *"The 38 Philosophies"* bonus CD by Michael S. Clouse.

Your Prospecting Toolbox

"Learn where to find two new
prospects every day—in
any city you choose!"

The Simple Art Of Duplication

"What you need to know to build
a business that duplicates!"

This program contains two
audiotapes, and features an
Art Jonak interview with
Michael S. Clouse.

MLMTrainingCentral.com
Build a Big Network Fast!

If you are looking for ways to recruit faster, keep your MLM representatives longer, hold powerful training meetings and build a long term residual business in Network Marketing, then you'll enjoy the training resources at MLMTrainingCentral.com.

Training tips on prospecting, sponsoring, training, self-development and business building skills. Free subscription to the **"MLM Leadership Report"** and lots of

moneymaking advice. Connect with expert trainers consultants, like Randy Gage and others. Learn the latest strategies to grow your Network and more . . .

How to Build a Multi-Level Money Machine
by Randy Gage

Discover how you can build your own multi-level money machine. *How to Build a Multi-Level Money Machine* is the first book ever published on the science of how to become wealthy in Network Marketing.

Randy Gage lays bare his exact system for creating a multilevel money machine. You'll find more money making tips on any two pages of this book than you'll find in the other so-called how-to books. It's packed with the actual methods, strategies and techniques you need to become wealthy in MLM.

You'll discover:

- What it takes to succeed in the business;
- How to get started fast and avoid common mistakes;
- Where to find the best prospects and turn them into distributors quicker;
- Counseling techniques to build depth in your group;
- Secrets to make your presentations more compelling; and,
- How to create a sponsoring "pipeline," that brings you a steady stream of new prospects.

Finally, you'll learn what to do once you have a large group; and the leadership strategies and management skills necessary to build depth and secure lines for lifetime residual income. **Get it today!**

www.NetworkMarketingTimes.com
Customer Service: 1 800 432 4243 or +1 316 942 1111

How to Earn at Least $100,000 a Year in Network Marketing
By Randy Gage

There's a reason this is the number one selling album in MLM history. It's the most intense, content-rich step-by-step training ever recorded for the MLM industry! You get 12 segments, which lay bare Randy's entire system from prospecting a potential distributor—to securing lines for walk-away income 250-plus levels deep.

You also get tapes on talking to prospects, building long distance lines, using tools to build faster, leadership strategies to build depth, how to do powerful meetings and much, much more. More importantly, you'll discover how to do this in a duplicable way so your key people can model your success.

Here's what you'll learn:
- How to recruit prospects faster;
- The secret to reducing dropouts by 80%;
- What to teach your new distributors in the first 2 weeks;
- Secrets of successful presentations;
- Conducting powerful, effective opportunity meetings;
- Building depth for walk-away residual income;
- "Driving" lines vs. "building" them;
- Advanced leadership strategies; and,
- Why your Network will only grow as fast as you do.

If you want to know the secrets to building a large, exponentially growing Network Marketing organization this album is what you want.

www.NetworkMarketingTimes.com
Customer Service: 1 800 432 4243 or +1 316 942 1111

THE FIFTH PRINCIPLE

"Is The Fifth Principle great stuff? Try this test: Buy 10. Give them to your people—even and especially your business prospects—and ask each of them to read it in 24 hours. (That's easy.) At the end of your current pay-period, subtract the costs of the books from the increase in your check. Use 10 percent of that amount to buy more books. Keep doing that for one year. Then do whatever you desire for the rest of your life."

—John Milton Fogg,
author *The Greatest Networker in the World*,
founder: greatestnetworker.com

1 book $15
2 – 9 books $10 each
10 – 49 books $8 each
50 + books - please call

Actual shipping
charges will be added
to these prices.

To order yours: visit www.nexera.com/v
U.S.A. 1 888 639 3722 International +1 425 774 4264

Notes